Adult Coloring
Quotes on Karma

This book belongs to:

Published By:

Amber Forrest

Website : www.amberforrest.com

ISBN: 978-81-943967-9-6

Hey... Thank You for being AWESOME.

We hope that you have fun time with your book. We have gift for You. You can download a free printable set of our best coloring pages by visiting our website :

AmberForrest.com

It would be so cool if you could share your completed images with us. You can tag us on

Facebook & Instagram
@ColorWithAmber

We are always working hard to improve our books. Please let us know how we are doing by writing a review of our book on your favorite online store.

Color Test Page

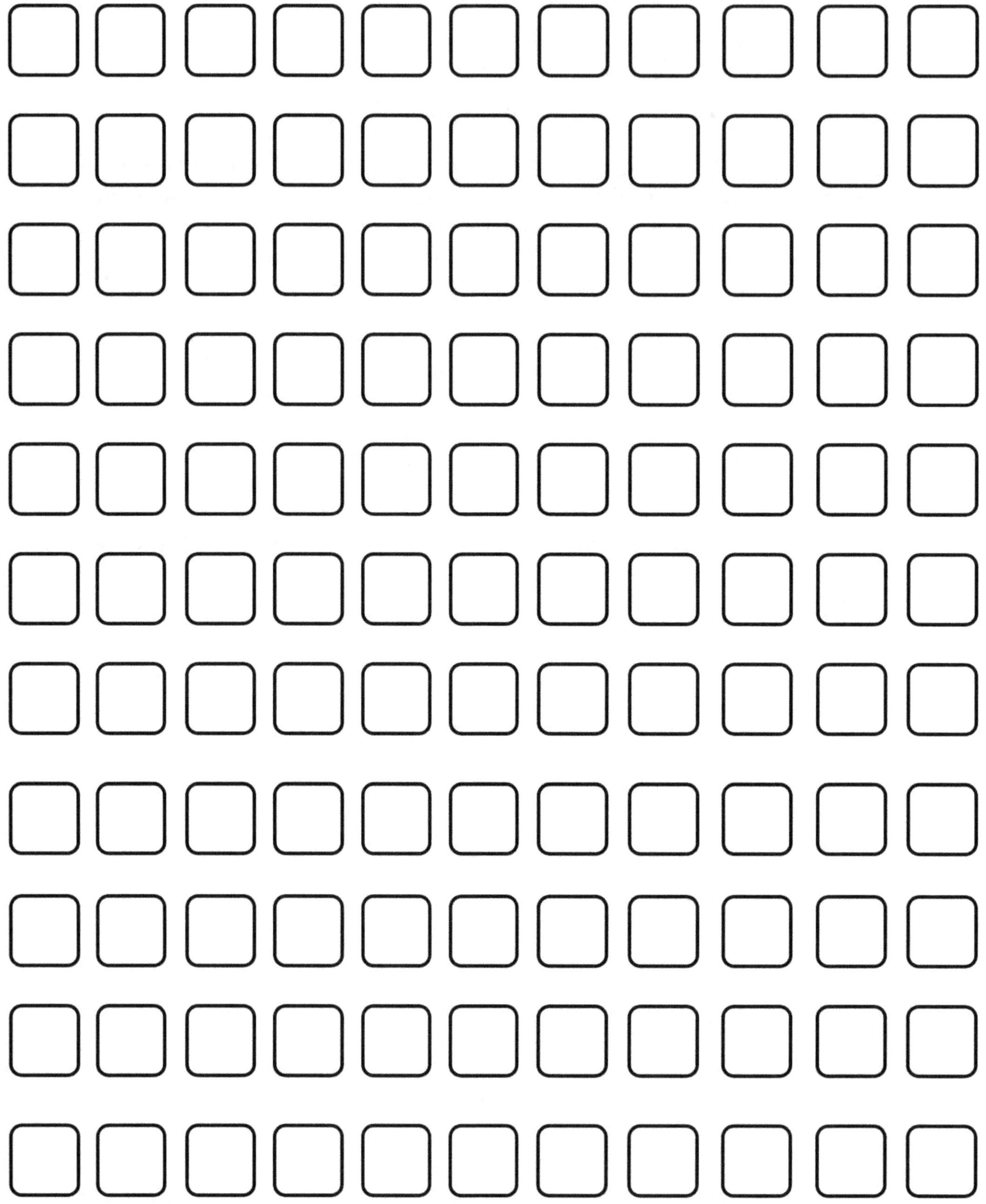

IT'S CALLED
KARMA
AND IT'S
PRONOUNCED
HA-HA-HA

KEEP
CALM
AND LET
KARMA
FINISH IT

DO GOOD
AND GOOD
WILL
FOLLOW
YOU.

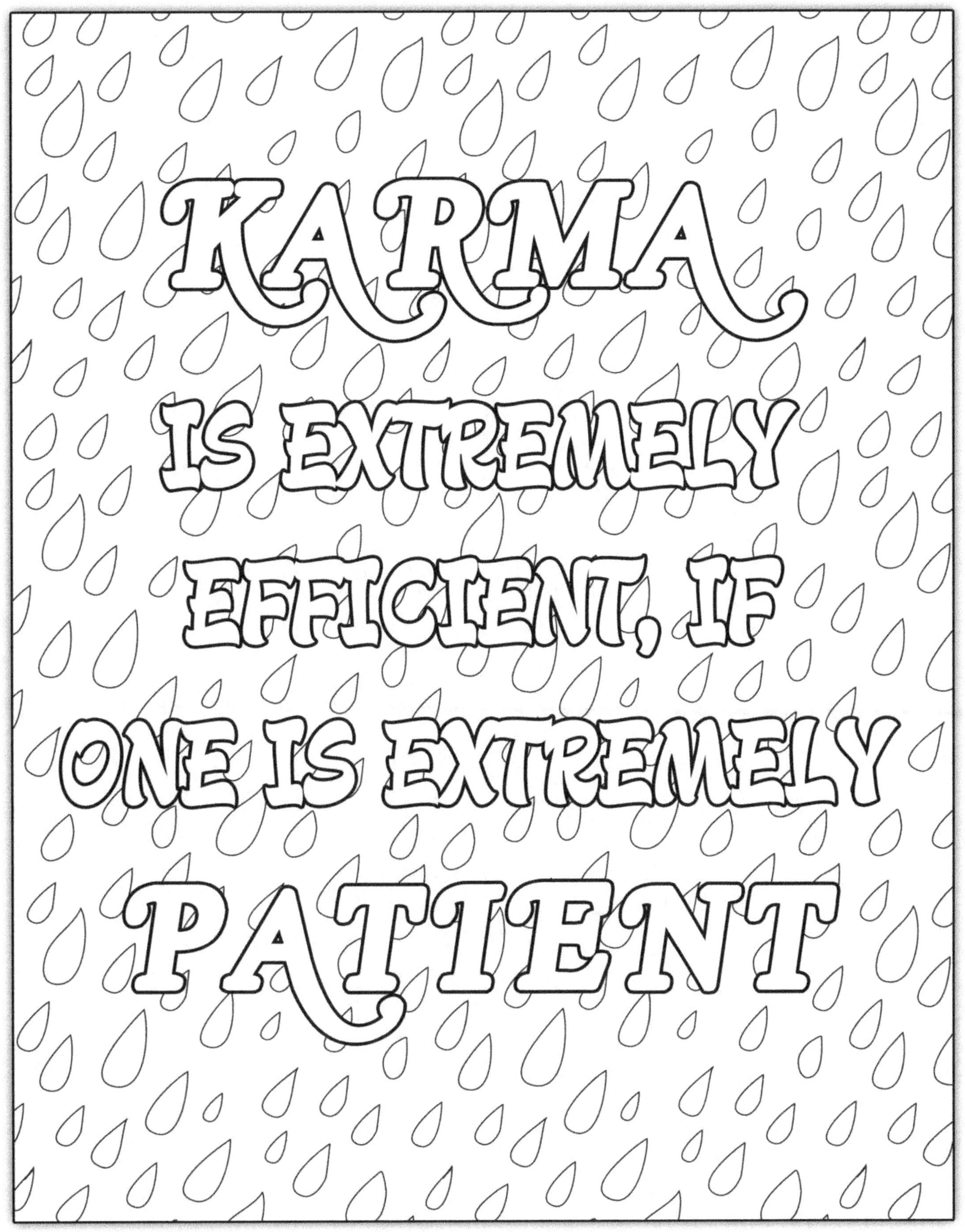

KARMA
IS EXTREMELY
EFFICIENT, IF
ONE IS EXTREMELY
PATIENT

IF KARMA
DOESN'T
HIT YOU
I WILL

EVEN DEATH
IS NOT TO
BE FEARED BY
ONE WHO
HAS LIVED
WISELY.

WITHOUT THE
KARMA
OF GOOD DEEDS
THEY ARE ONLY
DESTROYING
THEMSELVES

CHEATERS
ALWAYS WANT
YOU TO BE LOYAL
WHILE THEY'RE
BEING UNFAITHFUL

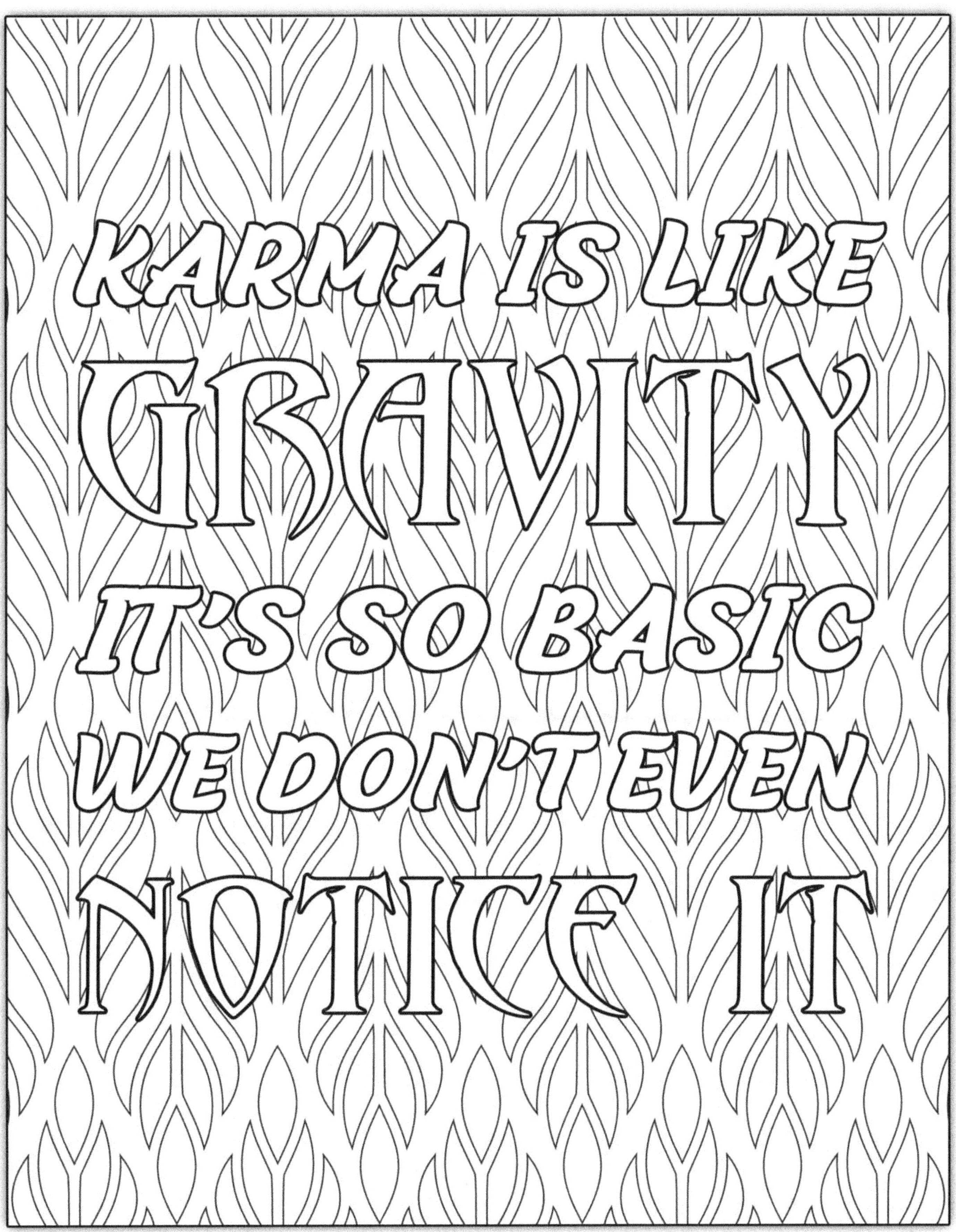
KARMA IS LIKE
GRAVITY
IT'S SO BASIC
WE DON'T EVEN
NOTICE IT

OUR LIFE
IS WHATEVER
OUR THOUGHTS
MAKE IT.
KARMA

PEOPLE ALWAYS ASK
FOR THE SECRET
TO SUCCESS
WELL, I'VE FOUND IT
GOOD KARMA

KARMA
I HAVE A LONG LIST
OF PEOPLE YOU
MISSED

NEVER LET
OTHER PEOPLE'S
ACTIONS DISTURB YOUR
INNER PEACE

NEVER LET ANYONE WALK THROUGH YOUR MIND WITH DIRTY FEET

THOSE WHO
ANGER YOU,
CONQUER
YOU.

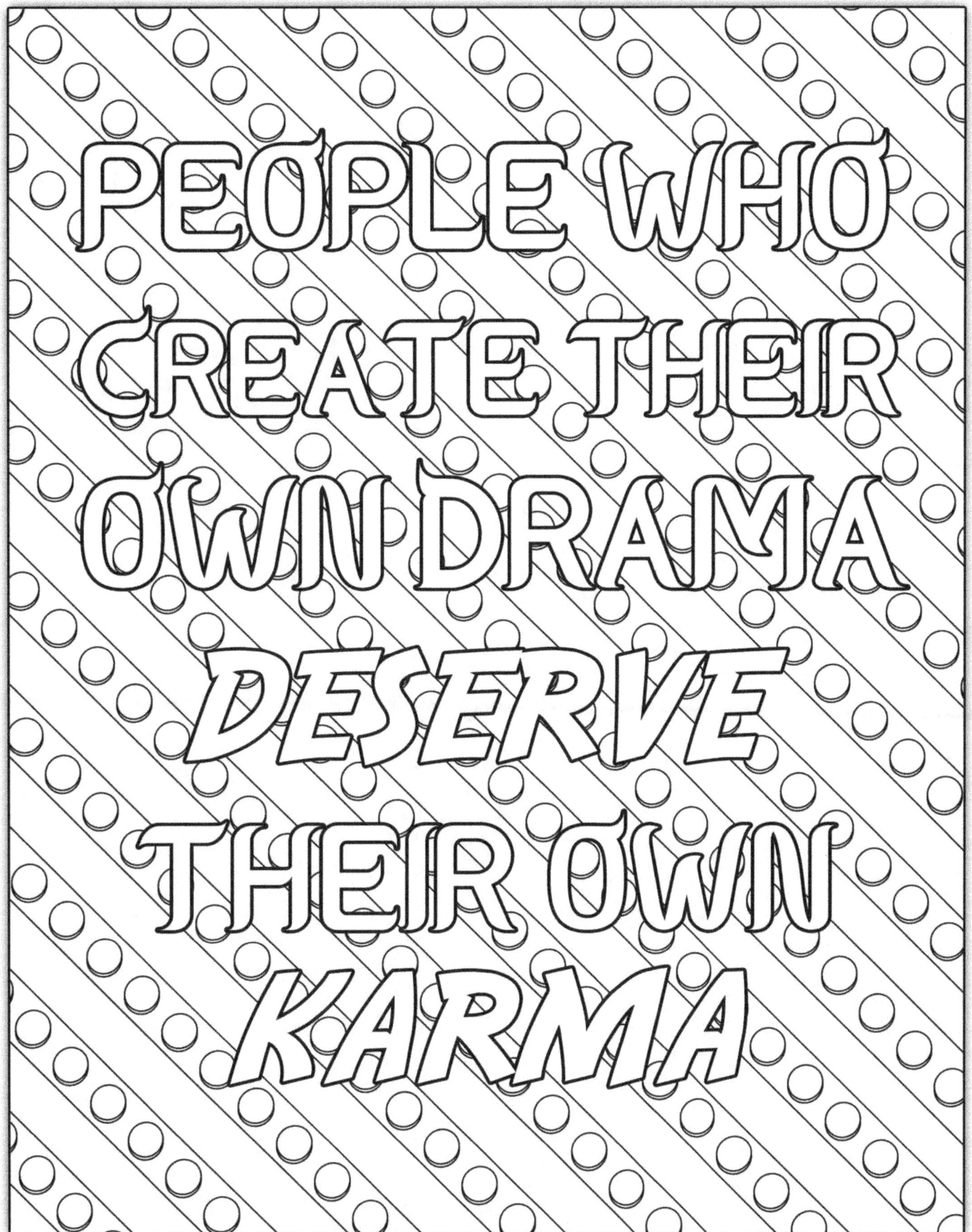

PEOPLE WHO
CREATE THEIR
OWN DRAMA
DESERVE
THEIR OWN
KARMA

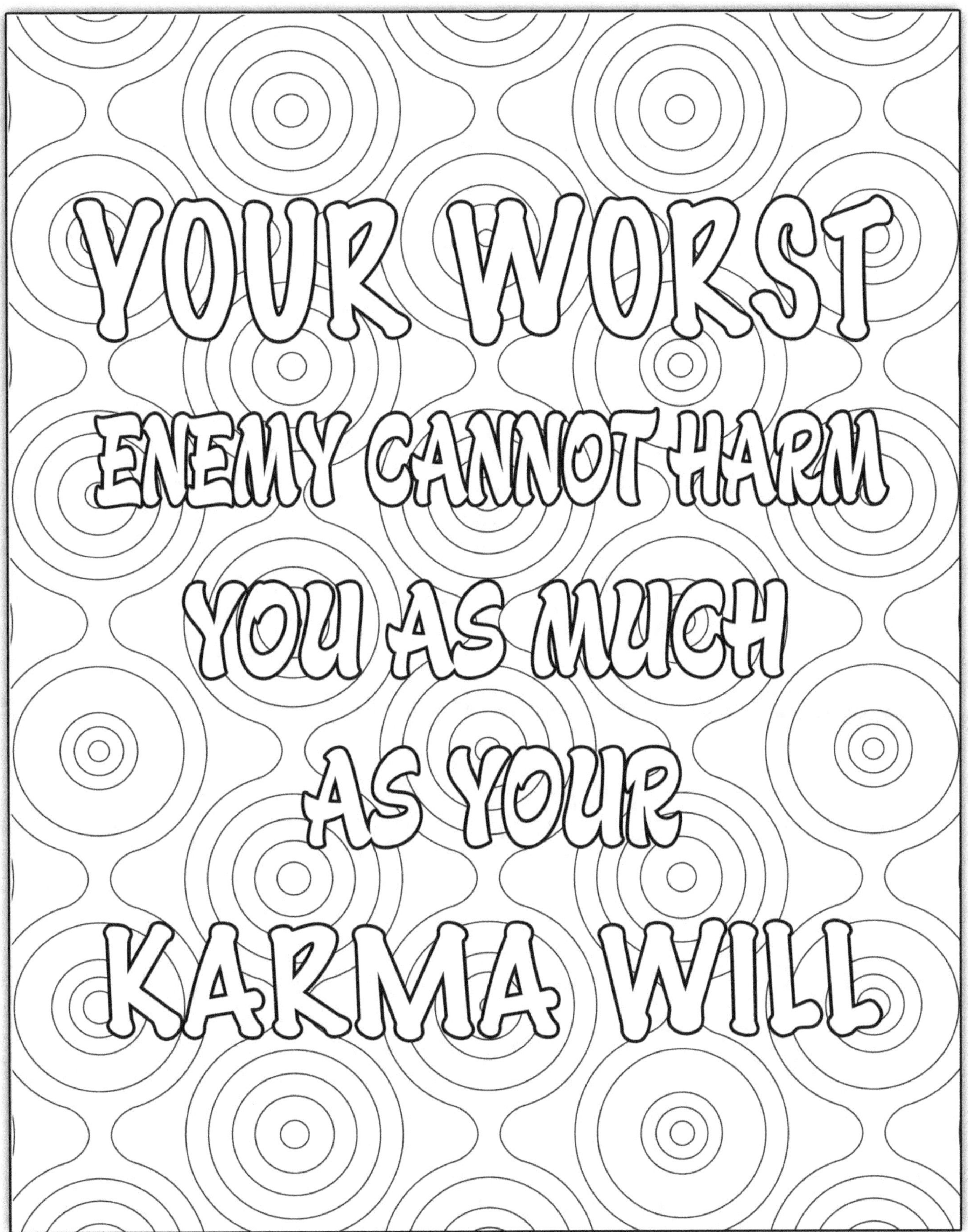
YOUR WORST
ENEMY CANNOT HARM
YOU AS MUCH
AS YOUR
KARMA WILL

KARMA
HAS NO
DEADLINE

GIVE OUT TO THE
WORLD
WHAT YOU MOST
WANT TO COME BACK
TO YOU

WHAT GOES
AROUND
COMES
AROUND

Sin makes
its own hell,
and goodness
its own
heaven.

I HOPE
KARMA
SLAPS YOU IN
THE FACE
BEFORE
I DO

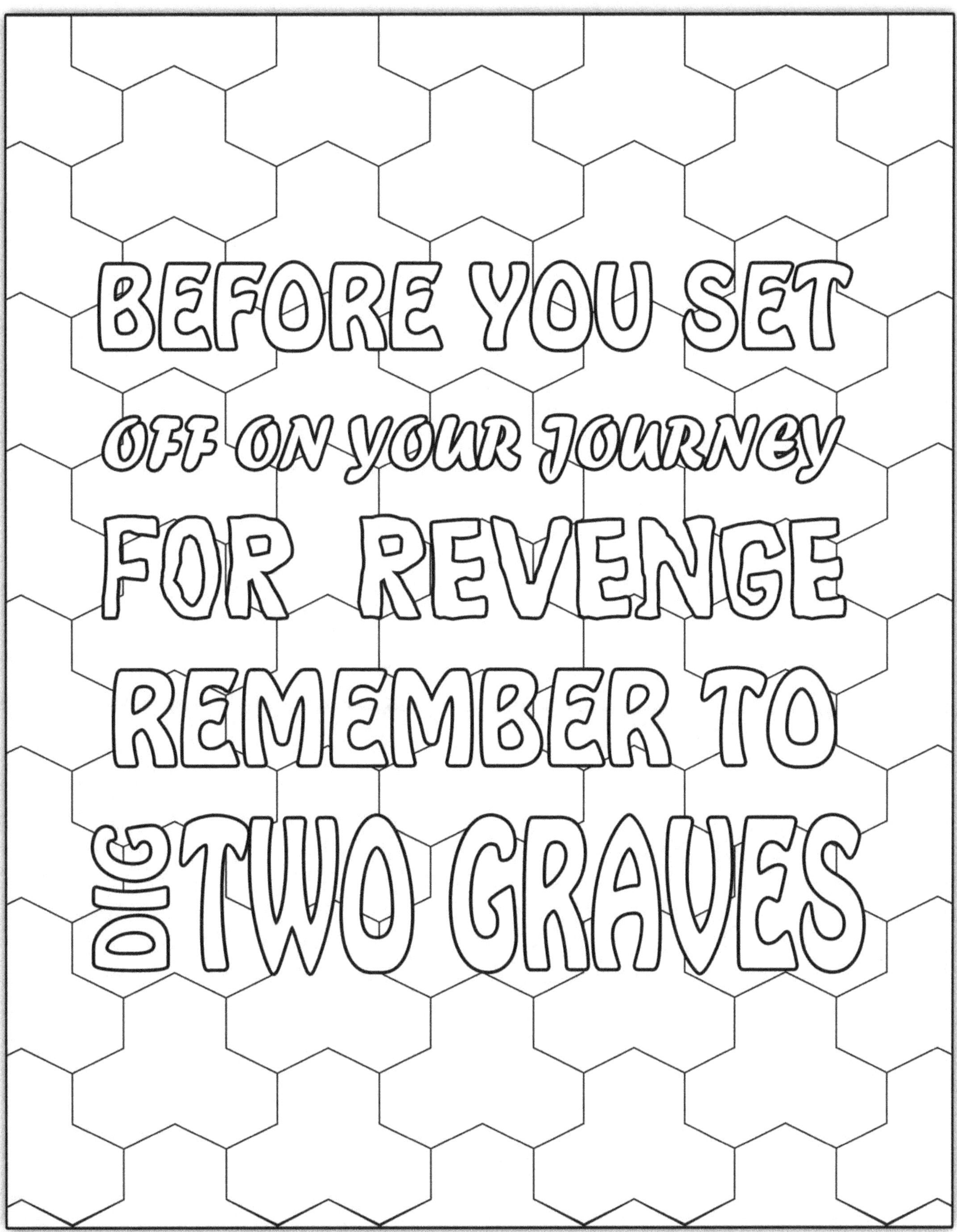

BEFORE YOU SET
OFF ON YOUR JOURNEY
FOR REVENGE
REMEMBER TO
DIG TWO GRAVES

WORTHLESS
PEOPLE
BLAME THEIR
KARMA

WHERE THERE IS
LOVE
THERE IS
LIFE

GO OUT
AND BE A
NICE HUMAN
BEING.

REVENGE
NEVER SOLVES
ANYTHING.
BUT
KARMA
WILL.

PEACE
IS IMPOSSIBLE
IF IGNORANCE
IS YOUR
MASTER

YOUR LIFE IS A
REFLECTION
OF EXACTLY
WHO YOU ARE.

TAKE
RESPONSIBILITY
FOR THE
ENERGY
YOU BRING
INTO A ROOM.

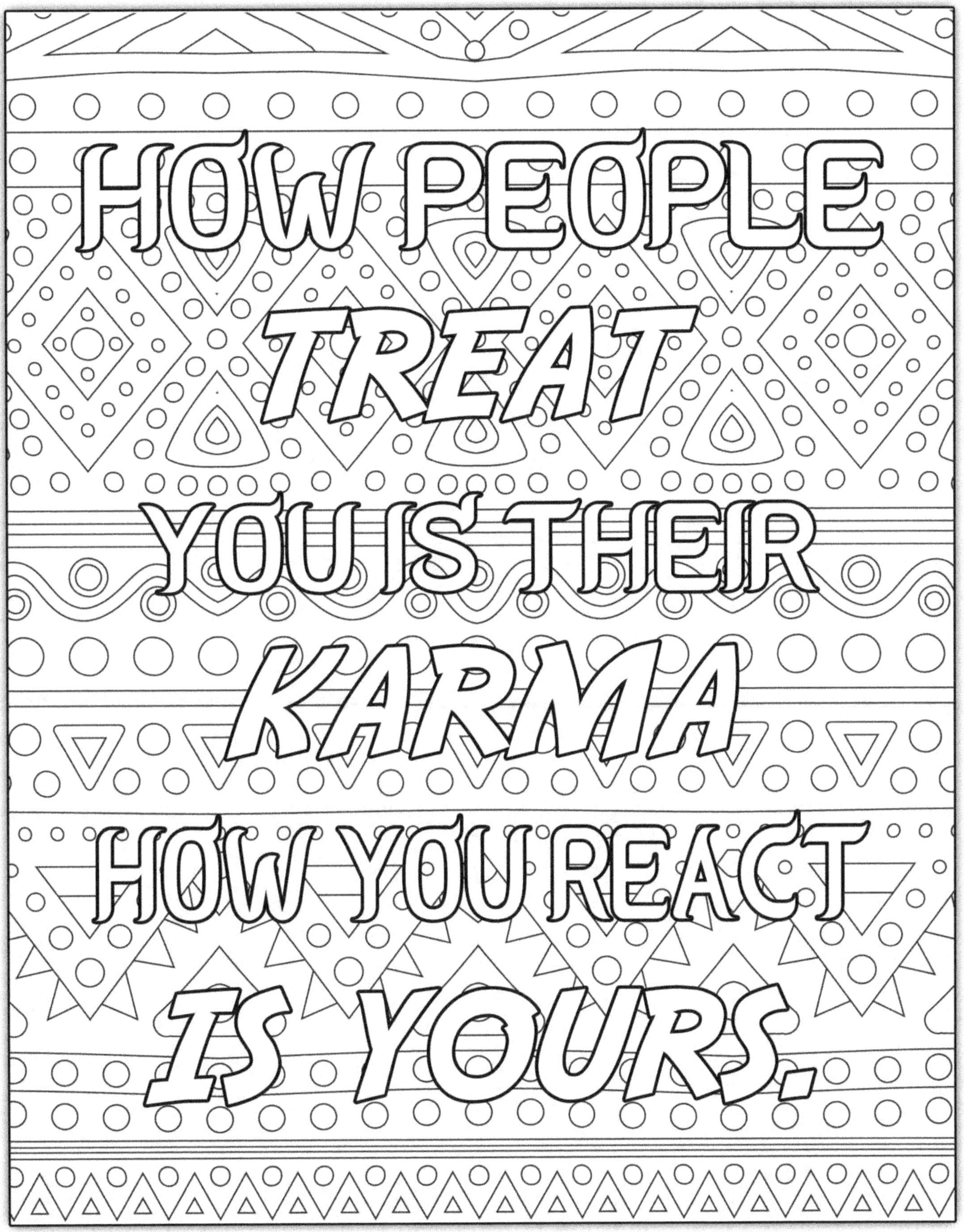
HOW PEOPLE
TREAT
YOU IS THEIR
KARMA
HOW YOU REACT
IS YOURS.

BE
MINDFUL
GRATEFUL
POSITIVE
TRUE
KIND

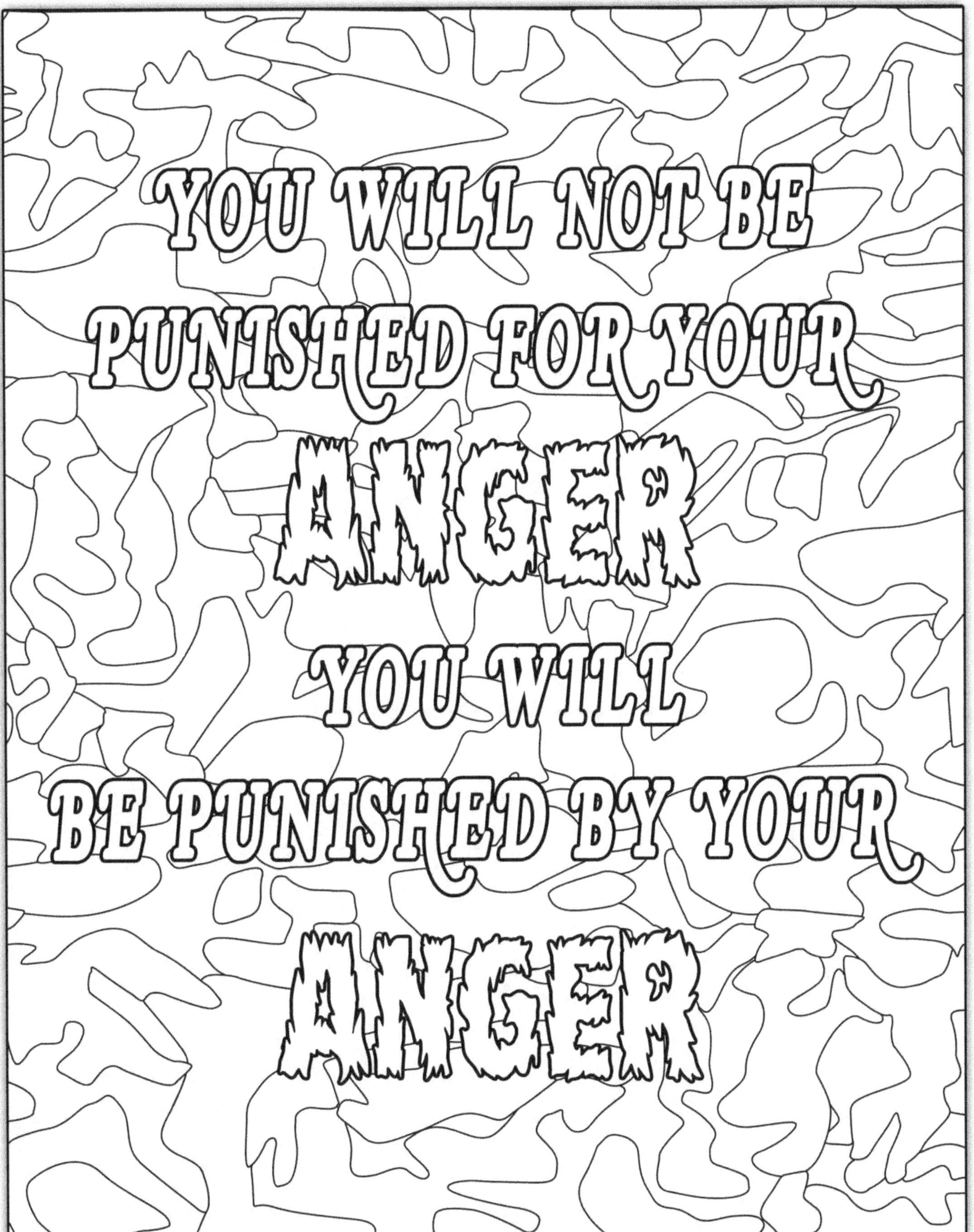
YOU WILL NOT BE
PUNISHED FOR YOUR
ANGER
YOU WILL
BE PUNISHED BY YOUR
ANGER

NOTHING IN
THIS WORLD
IS IMPOSSIBLE
TO A WILLING
HEART

SOMETIMES YOU
HAVE TO WALK
AWAY AND LET
KARMA
TAKE OVER

DON'T WORRY
KARMA
WILL
FIX IT!

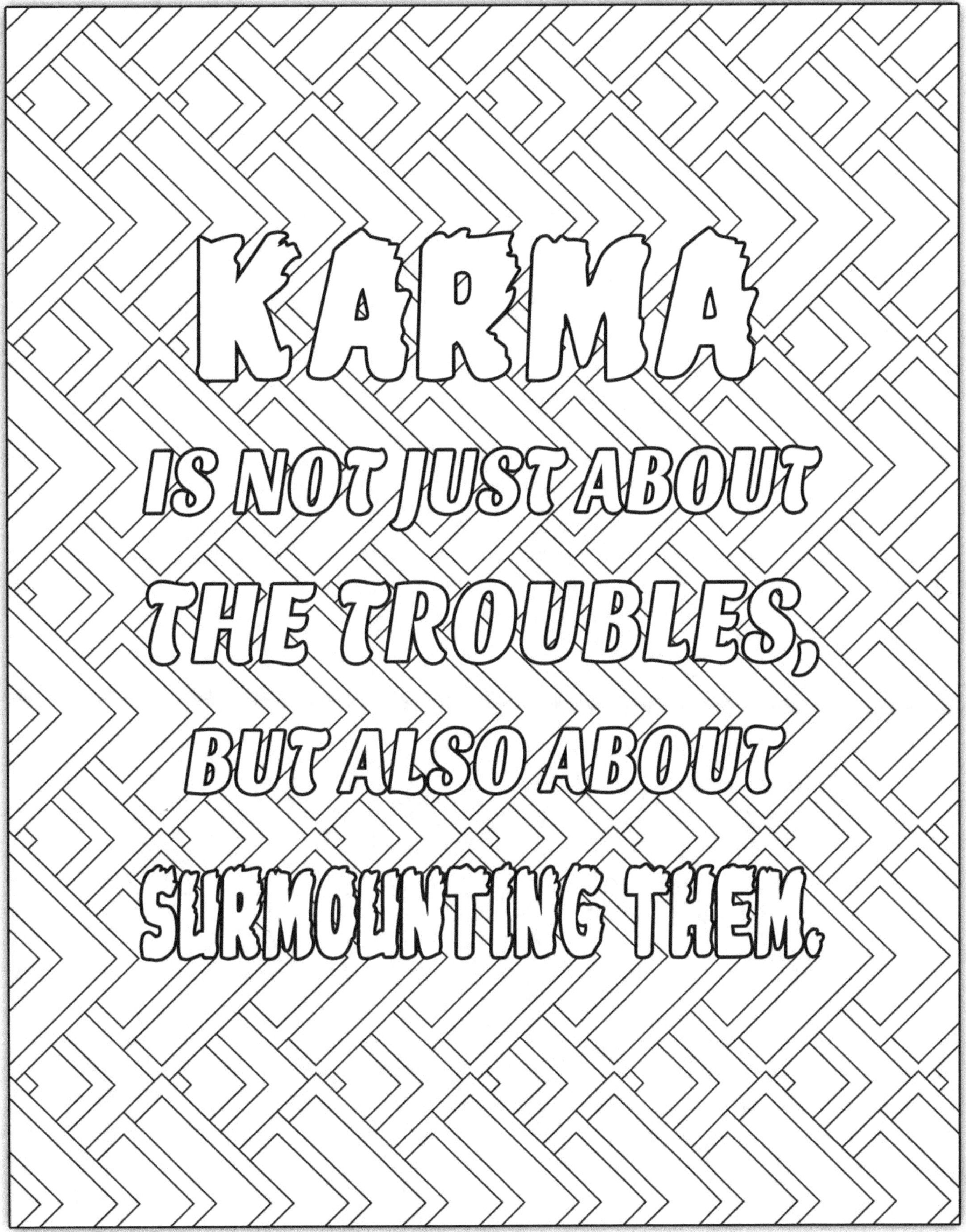

KARMA
IS NOT JUST ABOUT
THE TROUBLES,
BUT ALSO ABOUT
SURMOUNTING THEM.

THE BEST
REVENGE IS
ALWAYS TO JUST
HAPPILY MOVE ON
AND LET
KARMA
DO THE REST

I
SAW
THAT
KARMA

DON'T WORRY, EVENTUALLY EVERYTHING FALLS INTO ITS RIGHTFUL PLACE.

Thank you for buying this book.
Hope you like our work.

Please leave a review and let us know
What you think about our book.

For more books please check
Out our website :

www.AmberForrest.com

www.ingramcontent.com/pod-product-compliance
Lightning Source LLC
LaVergne TN
LVHW080515200726
843507LV00008B/1104